FIFTY WAYS TO TEACH BUSINESS ENGLISH

TIPS FOR ESL/EFL TEACHERS

MARJORIE ROSENBERG

WAYZGOOSE PRESS

CONTENTS

INTRODUCTION

When we teach business English, there are several factors to take into account. Many aspects certainly overlap with general English, but in general, the needs of learners are very different. There are a variety of topics that are necessary to meet learners' needs, and learners also need specialized vocabulary for the workplace in order to be successful in their jobs.

In general, business English is more task-related and goal-oriented than general English. The language we teach must be purposeful and is often priorities-based. As trainers, our job is to help learners with the vocabulary associated with their jobs and to find ways for them to learn it and use it confidently as well as opportunities to practice the communication skills that are so vital for them to achieve their goals.

This guide provides a variety of topics which can be adapted to different learners and their job situations and can be used with a variety of levels. Learners of business

English need language to carry out tasks, get ideas and opinions across, and in general, get a job done. Therefore, giving learners the chance to practice both language and communication / business skills in the classroom before they need it in the workplace is vital.

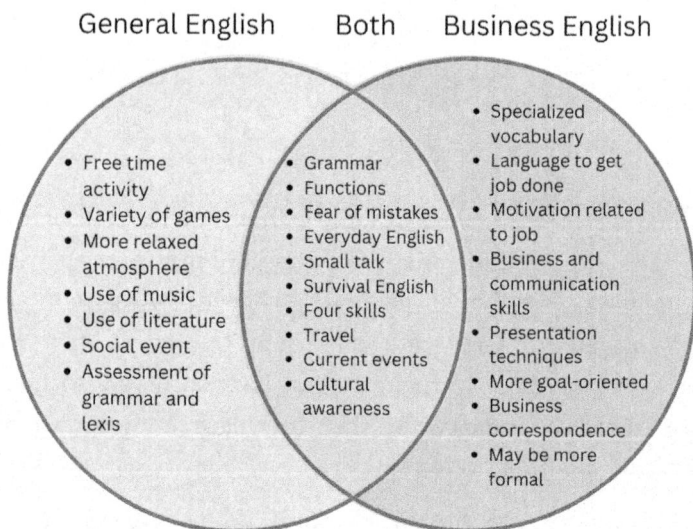

General English   Both   Business English

General English	Both	Business English
• Free time activity • Variety of games • More relaxed atmosphere • Use of music • Use of literature • Social event • Assessment of grammar and lexis	• Grammar • Functions • Fear of mistakes • Everyday English • Small talk • Survival English • Four skills • Travel • Current events • Cultural awareness	• Specialized vocabulary • Language to get job done • Motivation related to job • Business and communication skills • Presentation techniques • More goal-oriented • Business correspondence • May be more formal

We also need to take into account where a course is being held. Business English is taught in high schools that specialize in preparing students for the workplace, colleges, universities, private language schools, in companies, and in one-on-one lessons.

Depending on where you teach, the material may have a different focus.

For pre-experience learners, the emphasis may be on language about business and also consist of teaching general business concepts so that learners finish a course with an idea of how businesses are run. These tend to cover a wide variety of topics and may have to follow a particular curriculum. In addition, progress may be assessed through exams.

Once we begin working with people who already have jobs, the focus usually changes. In a language school there may well be a wide variety of topics with learners from different companies and fields, but the language will targeted to what the learners need for their jobs. In-company courses tend to focus on company-specific language and are often designed to help people do their jobs. There will likely be more input from the workplace, and lessons may change suddenly according to specific needs of learners.

Business English means teaching specific listening and speaking communication skills. Our learners' career success may depend on how well they can establish rapport with others, practice turn-taking and active listening, make use of critical thinking tools, and be able to explain and clarify ideas and concepts. They also need to give and ask for opinions, speculate and hypothesize, agree and disagree, and find ways to reach consensus in discussions.

Learners' needs in the other two areas of the four skills are also fairly specific: they need to read emails, memos, specialized texts, reports, proposals, websites, policies, and so on. Writing generally consists of the same sorts of workplace communication and correspondence, but in some cases learners may also need to learn note-taking or how to take minutes at a meeting.

The ideas in this book, therefore, cover a wide range of levels and topics. Some of them build basic vocabulary and simple communication, while others help more advanced learners expand their vocabulary and fine-tune their communication skills. They are adaptable to different situations and don't require a great deal of preparation. In addition, they are fun to do with learners and provide what the learners need when they need it. Each activity finishes with ideas for a **real-world follow-up** so that learners can connect an activity with the reality of their own work situation.

Throughout the years of teaching business English, I have found that the courses which were most successful were those that put the learners first and aimed to meet their particular needs while making instruction engaging and fun. Establishing rapport with the learners is also vital and helps groups to truly bond together creating an atmosphere of encouragement and support. This type of learning environment is what my learners have said has helped them to gain confidence, to enjoy learning, and to look forward to using English in real-world situations.

As a trainer, I find activities that encourage critical thinking and personal growth along with the essentials of the language turn out to be the most rewarding parts of lessons for both the learners and for me. Enjoy the tips.

HOW TO USE THIS BOOK

This book gives you different ideas for teaching business English and can be used by those starting out in the field as well as those who are experienced business English teachers and trainers.

The book is divided into eight major sections:

- Workplace vocabulary
- Business grammar
- Business writing
- Graphs and charts
- Communication skills
- Business skills
- Authentic materials
- Games and activities

You can certainly read through this from the beginning to the end, but not every activity will be relevant for the particular groups you are teaching. It is important to pinpoint what you need and look more specifically at those activities before looking through all of them. Obviously not every activity will work with every group, which is the reason for presenting diverse activities for different levels of learners and from different fields and specialties. However, you may find that you can adapt an activity to suit one of your groups, so it is worth having a look at what is offered here.

Here is a suggested method for using this book:

1. Read through all of the fifty tips without stopping.
2. Read through the tips again. Choose five or six that you think might work for one or more of your courses or clients. Decide when you will try them.
3. Choose different types of ideas, perhaps tips from different sections of the book.
4. Each time you use one of the tips, make a note about how well it worked for you and why. Remember that most of the tips will work best if you use them several times and adjust them for your teaching context. Don't try a tip only once and decide it's no good for your setting. Give the tips you try at least a few chances.
5. Every few weeks, read through the tips again, and choose some new ones. Discontinue using any methods that are not working for you after several attempts.

Finally, consider trying some of the other books in our *50 Ways to Teach* series. The series includes special volumes for teaching different skill areas, teaching online, using technology in the classroom, and becoming a 'greener' teacher. Improving your skills in these areas can only help you improve your overall teaching experience.

PART 1

WORKPLACE VOCABULARY

Teaching business vocabulary is not very different from teaching vocabulary for general English classes; the main difference is the vocabulary itself. Business English learners need specialized words that often don't appear in standard course books or even in ones written specifically for business English. Learners in BE classes also ask for authentic language that is used in the workplace and can be found in business English articles, websites, instruction manuals, etc.

For teachers using a coursebook, these ideas should provide supplementary activities that can be added to a lesson. For those who are not using coursebooks, these ideas can provide core elements that you can work on and expand as you see fit.

1

OFFICE ACTIVITIES

Level A2 – B1

Office workers need to be able to talk about their jobs and explain what they do on a daily basis. This activity helps them to find the vocabulary they need.

Ask learners to briefly describe their day in the office. In general, all levels of learners will run into vocabulary they simply do not know. Collect the words and phrases they need and then make them interesting and fun to learn.

Once you have a list of daily office activities such as

- answer the phone
- read and write emails
- file documents
- shred papers
- attend meetings
- work overtime
- show visitors around

- take part in conference calls
- punch in and out
- sort the mail
- use a USB / flash drive

and so on, go over them with the learners to make sure everyone understands the vocabulary. Then play a guessing game. Choose one of the activities and have the group ask questions such as, "When do you do this?" "How often do you do this?" "Do you need your hands, feet, etc. to do this?" until someone has guessed the activity. That person chooses another activity and the class asks the same questions until a number of the activities have been chosen and guessed. This can be done in groups in larger classes.

∽

Real-world follow-up: Have learners keep track of the activities they do during the week and report back on which ones they do most often or least often.

2

BEYOND THE BASICS

Level B1 – B2+

Working in a business environment also includes more advanced types of tasks. A brainstorming session with learners should turn up a number of phrases and activities that go beyond the basics. Some of these include:

- take minutes at a meeting and write them up
- set meeting agendas and distribute them
- cover for a colleague who is not in the office
- keep track of appointments
- work with spreadsheet programs
- give presentations, chair meetings
- use CAD (computer-aided design) programs
- design websites
- visit customers
- sell products or services
- deal with product launches
- submit expense reports, draw up business plans

Once these have been collected and written up on the board, ask learners to choose one that they do themselves, making sure that no two people choose the same activity by asking them to jot their choice down on a piece of paper so that you can quickly check them. In larger classes, it may be necessary to allow more than one learner to choose the same activity.

Then ask learners to move around the classroom to find as many others in the class as possible who also do that activity. When they find a match, they should write that person's name. Give learners time to mingle and practice the vocabulary. Stop them after 5-10 minutes (depending on class size) and ask how many each person found. The person with the largest number of names is the 'winner.'

~

Real-world follow-up: Have learners observe who does these activities in their work environments and report back to the class.

OFFICE SUPPLIES AND FURNISHINGS

Level A1 – B2

Many business people lack the basic words to describe the everyday equipment and furnishings found in the office. Brainstorm office supplies, write a list on the board, or show a presentation slide prepared in advance. Include items such as:

- shredder
- stapler
- paper clip
- hole punch
- calculator
- laptop
- staple remover
- USB/flash drive
- scanner
- scissors
- in and out boxes

- glue
- tape
- photocopier
- folder
- sheet protector
- swivel chair
- desk
- filing cabinet
- drawer
- coffee maker
- vending machine

Once the list is generated, ask a learner to make a sentence explaining what he or she uses one item for, but without naming the item: e.g., *I need this item to attach papers permanently*. The first learner who calls out *stapler* then makes a similar sentence about another items until most of the items have been practiced.

∾

Real-world follow-up: Learners note which of these items they use in a week and report back to the class.

SOCIAL ENGLISH MINI-DIALOGUES

Level A2 – B2

Social English is vital because we need to establish relationships with those we work with. Being able to answer correctly when spoken to or be able to express what you want to say takes practice, so it is necessary to learn specific phrases and responses. Learners can often prepare for these situations, but they may also come as a surprise when a guest suddenly appears or someone is sent on a business trip that wasn't planned.

Give learners a list of phrases and have them talk to a partner about the appropriate responses. They choose one or two good responses and write them down. Go through these with learners and agree as a class on the most useful ones. This list can then be sent to the learners as a document or an email to keep and to learn from.

There are a number of useful phrases and they might depend on the particular situation of your learners. Below is a suggested list but you might have others that you feel would be helpful to add or others may come up in class when you discuss these. It is also helpful to explain that because English does not have two forms of "you" there is no distinction between formal and informal language except by the use of first or last names and titles. Therefore, learning common phrases used in social English is very important for learners.

List of phrases and suggested answers:

A: How are you?
B: Fine, thanks. / Not so bad. / Don't ask!

~

A: What do you do?
B: I'm a banker/engineer/salesperson.

~

A: Thank you for all your help.
B: You're welcome. / Don't mention it.

~

A: Nice to meet you.
B: Nice to meet you, too.

~

A: Nice to see you again.

B: Same here.

～

A: Have a good evening.
B: You too.

～

A: Do you want a hand with that?
B: No, I can manage, thanks. / Yes, that would be great.

～

A: Would you like a cup of coffee?
B: Thanks, that would be lovely. / No, thanks, not right now.

～

A: May I join you?
B: Yes, please do. / Oh, I'm sorry, I'm waiting for someone.

～

Real-world follow-up: Have learners listen for phrases like these if they are confronted with English and bring them to class. This can go on throughout the course and be used to create a more complete list.

5

HOW DO I SAY ...?

Level A2 – B2

Learners often know what they would like to express but are uncertain about which words to use. Ask them what kinds of situations come up in which they have a need to express themselves in English and write them on the board or in advance on a presentation slide. These can be situations in which they already have phrases they are comfortable with and can share with others, or those in which they know what they want to say but don't have the words that they need.

Suggested situations and phrases:

- Arriving late for a meeting and apologizing: *I'm sorry I'm late, I hope you haven't been waiting long.*
- Offering help: *Is there anything I can do for you / help you with?*
- Accepting an offer of help: *Thank you. I would appreciate it.*

- Introducing yourself: - *Hello, my name is ..., and here is my card.*
- Picking someone up at the airport: *Hello, I am ..., from.... . I hope you had a good flight. Welcome to ...*
- Introduce a visitor to a colleague. *Jan, this is Sylvie. She's from the Swedish office.*
- Offering food or drink: *May I offer/bring you a cup of tea or coffee?*
- Not understanding what someone said: *I beg your pardon? Sorry, I didn't catch that.*
- Suggesting a break: *How about stopping for lunch? / How about a 5-minute break?*
- Finding a time to meet: *Would the morning or the afternoon be better for you?*
- Giving directions in an office: *It's the third door on the right / left.*

~

Real-world follow-up: Have learners watch a movie or a TV show in English and note down phrases they hear that are similar to these, then bring them to class and create a master list. Talk about when they are useful and in which situations.

6

TELEPHONING AND WEB CONFERENCING

Level A2 – B2

Business people often need to communicate on the phone or in web conferences. There are a number of phrases that they need in order to do this smoothly.

Give learners a list of functions and go over them to make sure everyone understands the situations. Then put learners in groups to brainstorm phrases they feel would be appropriate for each situation. Have each group read out their phrases and decide as a class which ones would be best to use.

List of functions and suggested responses:

Phone

Asking for someone on the phone: *May I speak to ...? / I would like to speak to ...*

Saying someone is busy: *He/she is on another line. / He/She is helping another customer at the moment.*

Saying someone is unavailable: *He/she is tied up at the moment. / He/she can't take your call right now.*

Asking someone to call later: *Could you call back later today? / Could you try again later?*

Telling a caller you can't hear them: *Could you speak up a bit? / I'm sorry, I can't hear you.*

Asking a caller's name: *Sorry, I didn't catch your name. / Sorry, could you repeat that?*

Asking someone to stay on the line: *Could you hold for a minute? Can I put you on hold?*

Saying who you are: *Speaking. / This is … (name)*

Explaining you will call someone back: *I'll get back to you later. / I'll call you back with the information.*

Web conference

Asking someone to join in: *Could you unmute yourself? Could you turn your microphone on?*

Asking someone to turn off their sound: *Could you mute yourself? / Could you turn off your mic?*

Asking someone to adjust their camera: *Could you focus your camera? / Could you adjust the lighting?*

∾

Real-world follow-up: Have learners make notes during the week of phrases they needed or heard on the phone or in a web conference and bring them to class so that they can expand their list of vocabulary and phrases.

GENERAL BUSINESS JOBS

Level B1 – B2+

Although companies may use their own in-house names for positions, a number of business jobs are standard and are used and understood by companies around the world.

Begin by writing several of these items on the board and asking learners if they know the jobs and if they know what the people in them do.

- Chairman of the Board
- Chief Executive Officer (this might be the same as Chairman of the Board in some companies)
- Chief Financial Officer
- Chief Information Officer
- Human Resources Director
- Research and Development Director
- Marketing Director
- Production Director
- Purchasing Director

- Sales Director
- Customer Accounts Manager
- Customer Service Manager
- Facilities Manager
- Project Manager

You can introduce vocabulary such as:

- *responsible for ...*
- *in charge of ...*
- *runs/heads the ... department*
- *is head of a team of ... people*
- *has to ...*
- *works closely with ...*
- *reports to ...*

Once the jobs have been made clear, let learners choose one and then have the others guess which job it is by asking questions, using the vocabulary above as a guide.

❧

Real-world follow-up: Ask your learners for their job titles and have them make sentences about their job duties using the phrases above.

HIERARCHY LEVELS

Level B1 – B2+

To describe our daily routines, we often need to talk about where we are within a company. Ask learners to look at the jobs in the list below and then, referring back to the jobs in Tip #7, put them together with the logical managers or supervisors. Possible answers follow the jobs, although some may fit into different areas.

- Personal Assistant (This position is found with any job in management; it is called a staff position as only one person is above the PA and no one is directly below.)
- Accountant (Chief Financial Officer)
- Software developer (Chief Information Officer)
- Recruitment Officer (Human Resources Director)
- Training Manger (Human Resources Director)
- Payroll Clerk (Human Resources Director)
- Engineer (Research and Development Director)

- Buyer (Purchasing Director)
- Sales Representative (Sales Director)
- Bookkeeper (Customer Accounts)
- Customer Service Representative (Customer Service Manager)
- Project Leader (Project Manager)
- Maintenance worker (Facilities Manager)

Introduce vocabulary such as:

- *report to*
- *direct reports*
- *oversee a team of ...*
- *responsible for ...*
- *on the same level as ...*
- *supervise*
- *run ...*
- *lead ...*
- *head ...*
- *work with ...*
- *above/below*

Have learners work in small groups and draw an organization chart based on a company they know or one they imagine. Ask each group to present their chart to the others and encourage the listeners to ask questions about them.

~

Real-world follow-up: Ask learners to bring in organization charts from their own companies or find an organization chart online that they can compare with what they have done in class or with the organization chart from their company.

9

LANGUAGE OF PAY AND BENEFITS

Level B1 – C2

The language of pay and benefits is very often the same throughout the business world. Learners need to know this language when they apply for a job or negotiate for better conditions, a promotions, or a lateral or upward move to another company.

Begin by asking learners what different types of phrases associated with financial compensation are found in the business world and have them make lists. Here are some words they might come up with:

- salary
- wages
- fees
- honorarium
- bonus
- raise
- expense account

- severance package
- pension
- commission

Clarify any of these that they don't know. Discuss the differences between these words and ask them which ones are used with the word "annual" (*salary / bonus / raise / pension*) or "hourly" (*wages / fees / honorarium*), "performance-related" (*bonus*). Clarify when employees are paid commissions, given expense accounts, given severance packages, and when they receive pensions/retirement benefits.

Then ask which words they know for benefits they might receive through their jobs. Here are some:

- stock options
- subsidized canteen
- pension plan
- medical plan / dental plan / vision plan
- maternity/paternity leave
- sick leave
- childcare facilities
- life insurance
- employee discounts
- company car
- flexible hours
- tuition reimbursement
- training courses

Clarify any of these that they don't know. Note that different countries and different companies have different words for some of these concepts. If you are not familiar with your learners' contexts and they don't know the correct terms, ask them to bring in literature from the Human Resources department if materials exist in English, or use a translator on the company website.

Ask if their companies offer anything else to employees and add these to the list.

Put the class into small groups and have them come up with a plan for financial and other benefits for people of different age groups and situations. Ask if there are other benefits that they feel would be helpful for these people. They then present their ideas to the class and discuss their suggestions.

∼

Real-world follow-up: Ask learners to report back on their own companies or companies they know about (without breaking confidentiality rules), mentioning the types of financial compensation people receive (without the actual figures) and the benefits the company offers.

10

SPECIALIZED VOCABULARY

Level B1 – C2

Specific situations often arise when learners need to work on a particular area of English, such as taking part in a meeting, visiting a client, giving a presentation in the company or to potential business partners, selling a product, interviewing someone for a job or being interviewed for one, etc.

First determine exactly what it is your learners need to do. Ask questions about the situation to gather all the necessary information. Once you are clear, you can begin to do your research. It may be that the vocabulary your learners will need can be found on a company website (either theirs or their partner's), in company brochures, in product information material, or in resumes and job descriptions, to mention a few.

Look through the material to determine where the vocabulary may be problematic and present it first to the learners. Discuss new or unfamiliar terms, and then read through the material you have chosen. As a final step, carry out a simulation using the material, with one learner taking on the role they will have to play and you playing the part of other person, or two learners in pairs. Check that learners feel comfortable with the new words and are prepared for the task.

Review some of the new words by asking your learners to explain them to you or in groups, or ask learners to describe what they think will happen during the meeting/presentation, etc.

~

Real-world follow-up: Ask your learners to report back on how the meeting/presentation/interview/visit went. Encourage others to ask questions about what happened and the language that was used.

PART 2

BUSINESS GRAMMAR

Expressing oneself correctly can help to get the job done, and small mistakes in grammar may cause misunderstandings. For this reason, working on problems and practicing specific structures can help learners with their communication skills. Specific structures have been chosen here to help learners express what they really mean and become more confident users of English in the workplace.

Remember that business English learners need the language to get their message across, and learning to use grammar correctly may be the key to doing this. Therefore, it is helpful to address specific issues that may cause problems, such as using the wrong tense or pronoun. When possible, let learners know how an incorrectly stated sentence could have been misinterpreted by someone else; this will help motivate them to practice the correct structures.

Learners also gain confidence when they have practiced structures and know how to use them. This feeling of confidence can help them feel more secure in the workplace when they have to use English.

11

DEALING WITH THE PRESENT

Level A2 – B2

Many learners are uncertain about the use of the simple present and the present progressive (or present continuous) form, as they often feel the present progressive "sounds more English."

Point out that the present progressive tense (*be* + - *ing* form of the verb) is sometimes called the "cell phone" tense because people use it to describe what they are doing when another person cannot see them (*I'm just walking up to the front door now*). In the workplace, we need this form to talk about actions or projects that are taking part at the moment but are not yet finished (*We're working on the budget report this week*), as well as for temporary actions (*I am taking part in a teleconference at the moment.*)

The simple present, on the other hand, is used when we talk about actions that take place regularly (*In the summer, the office closes an hour early on Fridays*). Since using the wrong tense can affect communication, it is important to spend some time working on these two tenses.

Ask learners to find some examples of ongoing projects in their jobs. Are their companies are currently implementing new processes, regulations, moving to another office, expanding operations, etc.? Have learners make sentences about these using the present progressive.

Next, contrast these with actions that they or their company always do. This can include daily routines, habits, or the general information about what the company buys, sells, produces, etc. Have learners make sentences using the present simple to describe these actions.

When they seem confident, ask learners to find a way to use both forms in a sentence. You can suggest the structure:

At the moment, we are ...-ing, but we
usually/often/sometimes ...

Note that learners should already be familiar with the adverbs of frequency, but they can also be reviewed here by brainstorming the ones the learners know, putting them in order from *never* to *always*, and then practicing using them in sentences or descriptions.

Stative verbs can also be introduced so that learners are aware of the verbs that are not normally used in present progressive. You categorize them in this way: possession (*have, belong to, own*), thinking (*think, understand, forget, remember*), feeling (*like, hate, love, need, want, wish*), and the five senses (*taste, smell, feel, hear, sound, see*). It may be helpful to have learners practice sentences using these verbs as well.

~

Real-world follow-up: Ask learners to make a list of ongoing projects at work as well as tasks they do regularly. They can report on these, and the class can decide if they have explained them using the correct verb form.

12

DEALING WITH THE PAST

Level A2 – B2

Many languages do not have similar tenses to explain the relationship to the past, so it is important to clarify the differences to help learners be clear in their communication.

Explain that the simple past tense is used when

- actions are completely finished: *I drove to work today.*

and the present perfect is used when

- the time of an action is unclear: *I've never taken the train.*
- repeated: *I've carpooled several times this year.*
- still going on: *I've had this car since 2021.*

Draw a timeline based on events in your life and practice questions with the group such as *When did you start your job?* and *How long have you worked at/in ...?*

Ask your learners to draw a timeline of important milestones in their own lives. Put them in pairs and have them ask each other questions similar to the ones you practiced with the group.

When they finish, ask them to report back on interesting information they learned from their partners. In this way you can monitor the correct use of the tenses, and making the grammar personal aids learners in remembering it. They can also practice using the structures *Have you ever ... (present perfect)? When was the first/last time you ... (simple past)?*

~

Real-world follow-up: Ask learners to talk about their last week or month in class using these two tenses. Other learners then paraphrase what someone else said to make sure that the meaning came across as intended.

13

SPECULATION USING CONDITIONALS AND MODALS

Level B2 – C1

Business people often use language of speculation to talk about future events while remaining neutral. There are times when they do not want to give opinions or to claim they have the answer to a problem. *(It would probably be better to fix a date today for the project launch rather than wait until we can meet again. / We could look into raising the unit price if we get information from the supplier soon.)*

Talk to learners about situations in which this type of language might be necessary. Ask them questions and let them respond freely without discussing language or grammar. Once you have several situations, you can begin to feed in the necessary language.

Introduce sentence starters such as

- *I wonder what would happen if ...?*
- *Do you think if we ...?*

- *Do you think we should ... ?*
- *Could we ...?"*
- *Do you think they may/might ...?*
- *We could ...*
- *... may/might ...*
- *If we ..., we could/would/might/should ...*
- *It would probably be ... if / rather than ...*

Work on the tenses and verb forms that follow these starters and help learners to choose between present and past tense verbs to complete them.

When you have a list of useful phrases using the correct form of the verb, choose a situation in the future that the group can then speculate about. In groups, learners hold a stand-up meeting in which they have a limited time to ask their questions and agree on a future plan. Stop the session when time is up (anywhere from 5 – 10 minutes) and ask them to tell the others what the problem was and the ideas they came up with. They should also report back on the language they used.

$\sim$

Real-world follow-up: Ask learners to be aware of times in their daily routines when they or another person needed to express speculation or offer suggestions using conditionals and modal verbs and report back to the class.

14

MORE MODALS FOR BUSINESS

Level B1 – C1

Much of the work in a business environment is focused on what someone must or has to do and conveying the message in a way that is polite and will achieve the desired results. Using these modals correctly takes practice.

Give learners these examples:

- *You must ...*
- *You have to ...*
- *You mustn't ...*
- *You need to ...*
- *You don't have to ...*
- *You don't need to ...*
- *You should ...*
- *You ought to ...*
- *You shouldn't ...*

Explain that:

- two of these are polite ways to give another person orders (*You have to ...* and *You need to ...*)
- two express something that something that is forbidden (*You mustn't ...* and *You shouldn't ...*)
- two express something unnecessary (*You don't have to ...* and *You don't need to ...*)
- two are suggestions (*You should ...* and *You ought to ...*)
- one is a very strong order (*You must ...*)

Ask learners when they might need these particular phrases or when they hear them. Put them in small groups and ask them to create a short dialogue to read aloud to the others who comment on it.

∼

Real-world follow-up: Ask learners to notice when they are told to do things at work. Ask them which language they would prefer if they were receiving the orders in English.

15

THE PASSIVE VOICE AND ITS ROLE IN BUSINESS

Level B1 – C1

The passive voice is used when an action is more important than whoever carries it out. It is also used when whoever carries it out is self-evident and does not need to be named. This form comes up quite often in business situations.

Write the following sentences on the board, and ask the learners what they notice about them.

- This car is made in the EU.
- These products are not being manufactured at the moment.
- Our company was sold last year.
- The new processes have been approved.

Ask these questions to help elicit responses:

- What do they all have in common? (The *be* verb and a past participle.)

- Do you know who or what carried out the action? (No.)
- Can you assume who or what was active? (Yes, we can make an educated guess.)
- Are they in different tenses? (Yes: present, present progressive, past, present perfect)

Work with learners to write out a procedure they are familiar with in 3 – 5 sentences using the passive voice. When they finish, they give them to another group, who rewrites the procedure using the active voice. As the agent carrying out the action can be assumed, they can simply decide for themselves who the agent is.

Ask learners to fold the paper so the original passive voice sentences cannot be seen and pass the active sentences to a third group who put them back into passive voice. The papers are then given back to the original group, which compares the two sets of sentences with the ones they had written. (Remember that passive sentences rewritten into an active form will often sound less natural. The two constructions are not the same, and each is used for a different purpose.) This exercise helps learners become familiar with different positions for the subject and object, not to tell them that the two forms are identical in usage.

∼

Real-world follow-up: Ask learners to notice any passive voice sentences they come across in their jobs, both in English and in their own language. Ask them to report on them in class and to give reasons why they think these sentences were in the passive and not the active voice.

16

ADJECTIVES, ADVERBS, AND INTENSIFIERS

Level A2 – B2

Ask learners if they know the different between adjectives and adverbs. Try to elicit the answer that adjectives describe nouns and pronouns, adverbs describe verbs, and intensifiers (such as *very, extremely, slightly,* etc.) modify adjectives and adverbs by making them stronger or weaker.

Brainstorm various adjectives and adverbs with the class, especially ones that may be used to describe products and services.

Ask learners to write the name of a product or service on a piece of paper. Then work in groups or as a whole class to guess what the product or service might be by asking questions using adjective or adverbs, such as. *Is the product environmentally friendly? Is the product large or small? Does it run smoothly?* etc.

Here are some adjectives to describe products:

- *adjustable*
- *comfortable*
- *electrical*
- *electronic*
- *practical*
- *portable*
- *sturdy*
- *translucent*
- *transparent*

Here are some common collocations:

- *battery-operated*
- *competitive price*
- *custom-made*
- *environmentally friendly*
- *fire-proof*
- *low maintenance*
- *mass-produced*
- *state-of-the art*
- *user-friendly*

Some intensifiers can be used with the adjectives and collocations above, but not all. Here are some examples:

- <u>*completely*</u> *adjustable, translucent, transparent*
- <u>*extremely*</u> *comfortable, environmentally friendly, low maintenance, user-friendly*
- <u>*fully*</u> *adjustable, electrical, electronic, portable, translucent, transparent*
- <u>*very*</u> *competitive price, comfortable, practical, sturdy*

These adverbs describe how a product works and would generally follow the verb such as the ones listed below.

- *efficiently*
- *quietly*
- *smoothly*
- *well*

Here are some verbs that can be used to describing how products work:

- *function*
- *heat / cool*
- *operate*
- *run*
- *work*

~

Real-world follow-up: Ask learners to choose a product or service that they sell in their jobs or buy themselves as consumers, and write up a short description of it using adjectives and adverbs.

17

REPORTED SPEECH

Level B1 – B2

Business people are often asked to report back on what was said in meetings or in written communication they received.

Begin by writing out statements such as the following:

1. He said, "I work from home on Tuesdays."
2. She said, "I am not writing the report at the moment."
3. They said, "We received the data last week."
4. She said, "I have already had lunch."
5. He said, "I will be in Berlin next week."
6. They said, "We are going to travel to a customer on Friday."

Go through them and ask the students what tenses the quoted parts of the sentence are in at the moment.

Answers:

1. present simple
2. present progressive
3. past simple
4. present perfect
5. will future
6. *going to* future

Then explain that reported speech means moving the main verb "back" one tense. Ask the learners what they think these tenses will become.

Answers: 1) present simple → past simple; 2) present progressive → past progressive, 3) past simple → past perfect simple, 4) present perfect → past perfect simple, 5) will future → would, 6) *going to* future → past progressive

Have learners come to the board to write the verbs in direct speech and then the verbs in the new tense.

Answers:

1. work → worked (*He said (that) he <u>worked</u> from home on Tuesdays.*)
2. am (not) writing → was (not) writing (*She said (that) she <u>was not writing</u> the report at the moment.*)
3. received → had received (*They said (that) they <u>had received</u> the data the week before.*)
4. have (already) had → had (already) had (*She said (that) she <u>had</u> already <u>had</u> lunch.*)
5. will be → would be (*He said (that) he <u>would be</u> in Berlin the following week.*)

6. are going to travel → were going to travel *(They said (that) they <u>were going to travel</u> to a customer on Friday.)*

Next put learners in pairs and ask each to write 4 – 6 sentences about actions that they may report on in their jobs. Learners exchange these with their partners, who then change the sentences to reported speech and write them down. Each pair then gives all their sentences to another pair, who put the reported sentences back into direct speech and give them to the original pair to check.

∼

Real-world follow-up: Ask learners to make a short list of things that were told to them in direct speech and report on them in class using reported speech.

PART 3

BUSINESS WRITING

Formal letter writing is not as common as it was before the widespread use of email but letters are still sent by companies to customers. However, emails, which have replaced many letters, also need to be written so that the message comes across and should follow the same structure as letters did.

In addition, learners need to understand and be able to use common structures for other pieces of business writing such as reports and proposals. They also need to practice writing concisely so that they can get their message across in a few well-written sentences, especially in memos or instructions for staff or co-workers. This section provides ideas on how to practice these skills.

18

A BUSINESS CORRESPONDENCE FRAMEWORK

Level B1 – B2+

Business letters and emails are written in order to achieve specific goals and address specific functions.

Write these typical features of correspondence (without the parts in parenthesis) on the board:

- Salutation / Greeting (beginning the letter or email)
- Reference / Subject (a few words to say what it is about)
- Inquiry (Asking a question)
- Request (Asking someone to do something)
- Information (Informing someone)
- Apology (Saying you are sorry)
- Regret (Explaining why you cannot do something you were asked to do)
- Closing remarks (Polite ending and thanking)
- Complimentary closing (Standard closing phrases)

Explain the different sections of a business letter using the information in parenthesis to explain the terms. Brainstorm possible phrases with the class so that they can fill in their framework to use for future situations in the office.

Suggested language:

- Salutation / Greeting (*Dear Sir or Madam, Dear Mr./Ms.,*)
- Reference / Subject (Account information / Invoice)
- Inquiry (*We would like to know ... , I am writing to ask you if/about ...*)
- Request (*We would be grateful if you could ... / Could you send us ... ?*)
- Giving information (*We would like to let you know that ... /We would like to inform you that ...*)
- Information about enclosures or attachments (*Enclosed / Attached you will find ...*)
- Apology (*Please accept our apology./We are very sorry that ...*)
- Regret (*Unfortunately we are unable to ... /I am afraid that we cannot ...*)
- Closing remarks (*I look forward to –ing. Thank you very much.*)
- Complimentary closing (*With best regards, Sincerely yours,*)

Once learners have some phrases they can use, ask them in groups to discuss correspondence they write and to think of other phrases that would be specific for their jobs. Check these in open class.

~

Real-world follow-up: Ask learners to bring a work email or letter (in English or another language) they have received which they can analyze with a partner and compare to the framework. Discuss any differences they discover while doing this.

19

FORMAL AND INFORMAL LANGUAGE

Level B1 – B2

Begin a conversation about formality and informality in the workplace and discuss the importance of knowing when to use both forms of communication.

In correspondence, it is important to use formal, less personalized phrases when writing to people that you don't know or don't know well. However, if someone is a long-term business partner, it is possible to use a different style of writing.

Start with the framework from Tip #18 and write out the parts of a letter or email on the board. The answers in parenthesis are suggestions; the formal phrases are first followed by the informal ones.

- Salutation / Greeting (*Dear Ms. Clark, / Hi Susan,*)
- Reference / Subject (*Arranging an appointment / Getting together*)

- Inquiry (*We are writing to inquire about ... / We'd like to know if ...*)
- Request (*Could you please send us ... / It would be really helpful to get ... *)
- Giving information (*We wish to inform you that ... / I'd just like to let you know that ...*)
- Information about enclosures or attachments (*Enclosed or Attached you will find ... / We've enclosed or attached ...*)
- Apology (*Please accept our apologies for... / I'd like to apologize for ...*)
- Regret (*Unfortunately, we are unable to ... / I'm really sorry that ... *)
- Closing remarks (*We look forward to your reply. / Looking forward to hearing from you.*)
- Complimentary closing (*Sincerely yours, / All my best,*)

Ask learners to work in groups to find as many phrases as they can for these functions, including both formal ones and less formal ones. Go over them with the whole class to make sure the phrases are correct and assigned to the correct definition. Point out that contractions are rarely used in formal correspondence but are common in less formal correspondence.

Finally, put learners in groups and ask them to write a formal or informal email, which they give to another group to change into the opposite style. Then put the two groups together to discuss the emails they wrote and the ones they changed.

Real-world follow-up: Ask learners to bring a formal email or letter they received as well as a less formal one to class so that the others can see them. Discuss the differences and the reasons for writing formally or less formally.

20

WRITING CONCISELY

Level B1+ – C1

Business people often need to write memos or instructions that must be clear and to the point.

Ask learners what kinds of things they write that others need to understand quickly.

Next, have learners brainstorm ideas to keep memos and other correspondence brief. Here are some that might come up:

- Don't elaborate unless it is necessary
- Avoid using long phrases or idioms
- Write in active voice rather than in passive voice
- Eliminate "filler words" such as *basically, really, very, just,* etc. and "filler expressions" such as *At the end of the day, needless to say, as everybody knows,* etc.
- Use only necessary adjectives; concentrate on the nouns.

- Avoid using the *There is …* construction
- Don't repeat information
- Be clear about the message you would like to get across

Give the learners this text:

As you all know, I will be on a business trip in Japan next week, and because we all know that the "early bird catches the worm," we need to ensure that our department is one of the first ones to finish our annual report. Reports on our sales figures are being finalized this week, however, so we may not have all the necessary information we need to finish it. If that is the case, please let me know and I will do my best to get the information to you so you can finish it off. There is always a way to find missing information, and I am sure that I will be able to help with this. Please let me know by the beginning of next week if you will be able to finish our report so that we can send it to the board of directors. And let me know if there is a problem getting this done so that I can come up with another solution. [170 words]

In groups, learners look at the text and discuss any "mistakes in being concise" that they see and determine what they think the main message is (writing an annual report by a deadline). Then ask them to rewrite it to make it shorter.

Possible answer:

I will be away next week so would like you to finish our annual report. If you do not have the sales figures you need, let me know so I can get them to you. I need to see the report by Monday so I can forward it to the board. Please let me know if this is possible. [59 words]

∼

Real-world follow-up: Ask learners to look for both concise and wordy pieces of correspondence they receive at work. They can bring them to class so that others can see them and discuss them.

21

WRITING REPORTS AND PROPOSALS

Level B2 – C1

Reports and proposals generally follow a specific format, which helps learners to write in an organized way.

Give these section heads to the learners and ask them to put them in the correct order:

- Conclusion
- Title
- Introduction
- Recommendations
- Findings

Answer: Title, Introduction, Findings, Conclusion, Recommendations

Ask learners how long they think the various sections should be for short reports.

Answers:

- **Title:** Just the most important information explaining what it is about.
- **Introduction**: One or two sentences
- **Findings**: Several sentences that describe the situation. One paragraph or sentence to explain what the writer has learned, and one paragraph to further elaborate and possibly give an opinion.
- **Conclusion**: One or two sentences
- **Recommendations**: One or two sentences

Brainstorm useful phrases with learners that would fit into the different sections of the report and write them down to create a framework and language they can use.

Possible answers:

Title: *Report on ...*

- **Introduction**: *This reports aims to ... / The aim of this report is to ... / This reports sets out to ... / The purpose of this report is to ...*
- **Findings**: *It was discovered that ... / Research into the matter showed that ... / We found out that ... However, ... could happen / It might be possible to ... / If things continue as they are, ... I think that ...*
- **Conclusion**: *At the moment ... / At present ...*
- **Recommendations**: *It is recommended that ... / I would recommend ...*

Have learners in groups choose a topic they can write a report on and then write the report. Assign a number to each group and hang the numbered reports up around the classroom. Then learners walk about and read them, making notes using the numbers on the reports to express how clear they found them and how the practiced language was used. Discuss possible improvements or use reports as examples for others to follow.

∽

Real-world follow-up: Ask learners for reports they have written or received at the workplace and compare them to this framework to find similarities and differences.

PART 4

CHARTS AND GRAPHS

Data and figures are often presented visually in business, as they are easier to understand that way and often take less time. There are several types of charts and graphs that are commonly used, and it is important for learners to know when to use each type and what their purposes are. In addition, learners need the language to talk about them so that they can explain them to others or understand what another person is telling them.

This is in a separate section as it is very specific language and is normally used to describe economic indicators, trends, or other type of data. The language itself is used across a wide range of businesses and industries as it is not dependent on a particular area but is common to all. As there is a fair amount of language for learners to become familiar with, it is essential to give them time to work on these specialized words and phrases.

22

TYPES OF CHARTS AND GRAPHS

Level B1-B2

Begin by drawing three types of graphs on the board. Tell learners that one is a line graph, one is a pie chart, and one is a bar chart; and that one shows percentages of a whole, one compares similar items, and one shows development over time. Ask them to put this information in the correct place.

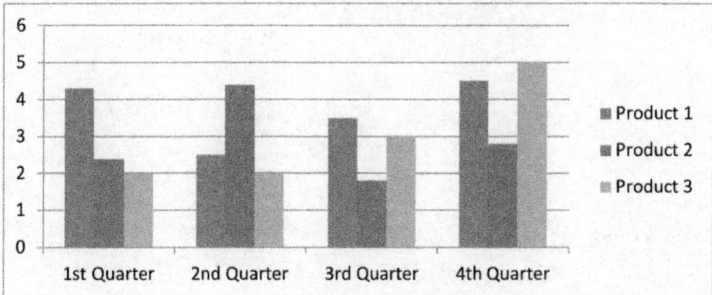

graphic #1

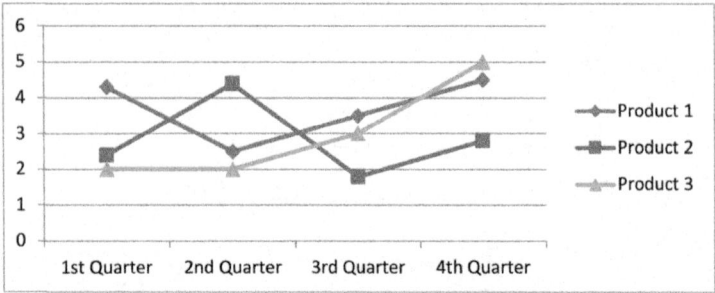

graphic #2

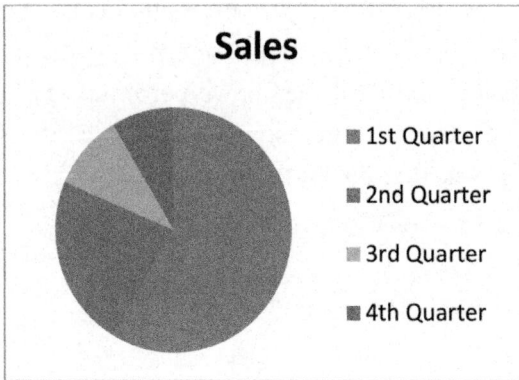

graphic #3

Answers:

1. Bar chart – compares similar items
2. Line graph – shows development over time
3. Pie chart – shows percentages of a whole

Next, give leaners these terms:

- segment
- vertical axis
- shaded area
- dotted line
- bar
- percentage
- horizontal axis

and ask them to assign them to the correct chart.

Answers:

1. Bar chart – column, bar
2. Line graph - vertical axis, dotted line, horizontal axis
3. Pie chart - segment, shaded area, percentage

Finally, ask learners to give examples of when they think each of these charts might be used.

Possible answers:

- **Bar chart**: sales volume for a different articles in a product line, stock of different products over a period of time
- **Line graph**: development of sales, change in interest rates
- **Pie chart**: percentages of number of employees in certain demographics (ages, gender, etc.) in a

company, percentages of items produced

~

Real-world follow-up: Ask learners to bring materials from their job which use any of these charts and have them explain the data behind them to the others.

23

WORDS OF MOVEMENT

Level B1+ – B2

English has a number of words that describe movement in a line graph, and it is helpful for learners to be familiar with them.

Ask learners to draw a table with five columns using these expressions at the top of the column:

- upward movement
- downward movement
- reaching the top
- reaching the bottom
- staying the same

Then call out a few words and phrases such as *fall* (downward movement), *remain stable* (staying the same), *peak* (reaching the top), *rise* (upward movement), *bottom out* (reaching the bottom) and ask learners where they think they go, checking to make sure they put them in the correct columns.

Then ask learners to call out words they know and add them to their lists, checking first that everyone knows where they belong. When you have several words in each column, ask learners to mark them as nouns or verbs and try to find the noun or the verb that belongs to the word they have.

Next ask learners to draw a second chart with these two titles for the columns: "words indicating speed" and "words indicating size." Again call out a few words such as *significant* (size) and *quick* (speed). Ask them to think of more adjectives which could be classified in this way by calling them out in class. Once they have several words in the table, have the learners make adverbs from the adjectives.

When the learners have both tables filled in, ask them to make sentences using the verbs from the first column with appropriate adverbs and the nouns with appropriate adjectives.

∽

Real-world follow-up Ask learners to find a line graph from their own company and bring it to class. Ask them to describe it to the others using the vocabulary they have learned.

24

EXPLAINING LINE GRAPHS

Level B1+ – B2

Tell learners to each draw two blank line graphs with the horizontal axis showing the 12 months of the year and the vertical one showing monetary figures from $1,000 to $10,000, with a mark for each increase of $1,000. Then ask them to each draw a line graph with two lines indicating sales of two different products over the period of one year.

Put learners in pairs and have them sit back-to-back. Each learner explains his or her line graph to his or her partner using as much of the vocabulary they learned in Tips #22 and #23 as possible. The partner draws the graph without seeing it but may ask questions. When they finish, they compare the graphs that were drawn with the original graphs.

Ask the learners to note the language that was used and then expand on it so that they increase their vocabulary when talking about line graphs.

Real-world follow-up: Ask learners to find a line graph online or in a newspaper, etc., and to write a description of it. They could practice with a partner by explaining these graphs to each other.

PART 5

COMMUNICATION SKILLS (SOFT SKILLS)

Most business people agree that soft skills are necessary to be successful in the workplace, and the success of a career often depends on how well people master these interpersonal skills. They are often taught in the first language of the learner, but teaching them in English provides the learners with additional practice as well as vocabulary relating to the specific skills.

These skills are seen as positive attributes in the workplace because they help to establish and maintain personal relationships. In many cultures, being able to communicate well is the key to success and can lead to increased business and understanding among business partners. These skills are important for pre-experience learners, since mastering them can help them at job interviews, and are, of course, vital for those already active in the workplace.

25

GETTING YOUR MESSAGE ACROSS

Level B1 - C1

Draw a pie chart on the board with these percentages on it and explain that this is a communication model devised by psychology professor Albert Mehrabian in 1971. Ask the learners what they think the numbers represent in terms of trying to get our message across.

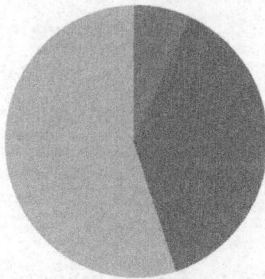

7%, 38%, 55%

After letting learners discuss this, give them the hint that the three areas refer to our tone of voice, the words we say, and our body language, and ask them which they think is which.

Finally, tell them that according to Mehrabian, the messages we communicate are made up of 55% body language, 38% tone of voice, and 7% actual words. Ask them what they think of this and if they think it is true or not. More advanced groups can be asked to give examples to back up their opinions.

Put learners in groups and have one of them give a short talk to the others. Tell the speaker to make use of their voice and body language to get the point across. Then debrief the group and ask them what they remembered of what the speaker said, and if they were influenced at all by the tone of voice and the body language.

Then ask the speaker to move to a different group and repeat the exercise, this time using a different tone of voice and different body language that is not consistent with the words, and debrief again. Ask the second group of learners what they understood from the short talk and compare the results with those of the first group.

∿

Real-world follow-up: Ask learners to notice if they are confronted with situations in the workplace in which the tone of voice or the body language does not match the words that are said. If so, ask them to report on how they felt about it.

26

ESTABLISHING RAPPORT

Level B1 – C1

Ask learners how they feel when they are with someone who they feel understands them, as opposed to someone who they feel does not see their point of view. Ask them to explain if they are comfortable or not, and if not, why not.

Tell them that various aspects go into establishing rapport which is a feeling of understanding between people. These include paying attention to:

- body language
- speed of speech
- tone of speech
- gestures
- eye contact
- posture
- type of language used (use of slang)
- register (formal or informal language)
- breathing patterns

- physical distance between speakers

Explain that when we want to make another person feel comfortable and taken seriously, we often have to try to match several of these factors, although some such as posture, gestures, body language, and even speed and tone of speech may be easier than things such as breathing patterns and language.

Tell the learners they are going to try the "three-minute exercise." Put learners into groups of three. Assign one to be the speaker, one the listener, and one the time-keeper. The time-keeper should sit so that they can see the speaker.

Tell the speaker to start telling a story to the listener, who matches posture, gestures, body language, etc., and responds with verbal sounds of interest but no specific language.

After one minute, the time-keeper gives a signal, and the listener begins to mismatch posture, gestures, body language, eye contact, etc. The listener, however, can continue to use verbal responses of interest. This phase also lasts for one minute, until the time-keeper gives the signal again and the listener returns to the original position of matching body language and using verbal cues of interest.

After one more minute, stop the group and debrief. Ask the speaker how they felt, and if they thought the listener was paying attention and why or why not. Ask the listener as well how it felt both matching and mismatching. Explain that this short exercise is an example of how we can both establish and break rapport with another person. Open this up to a class discussion of why this is important knowledge for the workplace.

~

Real-world follow-up: Ask learners to observe themselves as well as others and the use of rapport or the lack of it in the workplace. Ask them if they have noticed how they feel when they think the person they are in a conversation with isn't listening and when the other person is listening carefully. Have them describe what they have seen among their colleagues or how they feel about this themselves.

27

PERSUADING OTHERS

Level B2 - C1

This is an important skill to have in the workplace, both for meetings and on the phone. The first step is often to match the tone of voice as well as the speed of speech of the person you are speaking to. If someone is upset or angry, "meeting them in the place they are in" by matching the tone and speed can help you to establish rapport with them and eventually move on to the next part of the conversation.

Ask learners to give you some sentences that people might say when they are upset and the types of sentences people use to answer these. Put learners in small groups. Ask one to say an angry sentence and the next person uses a calming response but in the same tone of voice. Then ask the second person to slowly use a calmer tone of voice and possibly a slower pace of speech to continue the conversation. Ask the groups for feedback on whether it was then easier to continue the conversation and what those involved in speaking, as well as the observers, noticed.

Explain that this is step one and allows a conversation to take place. Explain that the goal of persuasion is generally to reach a goal, but often the goals of the people involved differ.

Continuing in small groups, tell the learners that once they have established the possibility of carrying on a productive conversation, they should come up with a typical workplace situation and fix two different goals for the outcome they would like. Have the group brainstorm creative ways to overlap the goals so that they can begin to work on one that is beneficial to all. Look at the goals from the point of view of both people and come up with reasons to find a solution. Imagine what the other person might have against your idea and try to think of counter-arguments. Discuss different possibilities in the group. Then debrief and ask for feedback from the groups on how the exercise went. If at any time the tone of voice or the speed of speech changes, making discussion difficult, learners should again try to match these and slowly bring the conversation back to a calmer and more collaborative discussion.

❧

Real-world follow-up: Ask learners to report on similar situations in the workplace and how they or others responded to co-workers or bosses when a useful conversation seemed difficult to achieve.

28

MAKING COMMUNICATION AS CLEAR AS POSSIBLE

Level B2 – C1

Miscommunication can lead to misunderstandings in every situation, and in the workplace these can have a very negative effect.

Ask learners for examples of when something was communicated to them that they understood well, and then examples of when they didn't understand what they were being told. With the class, analyze the elements that made up the communication.

Ask these questions:

- Did the person plan in advance what they wanted to achieve? How did you know this?
- Did the person plan in advance what they wanted to say? Can you give an example?
- Was the person concise? Can you give an example?

- Did the person give specific examples to make their point? What did they say?
- Do you think the person took their audience into account? How do you know this?

Put learners in small groups and ask each to come up with a suggestion or proposal that might be helpful in the workplace. Have them work through the five questions above to prepare a short speech on this. Ask one person from each group to give their talk to the whole class. Then ask the class if they achieved their goal, and discuss the points they were to take into account as well as general feedback.

∼

Real-world follow-up: Ask learners to notice such conversations in the workplace and report those they took part in to the class. They can use the checklist in the tip to give specifics on the conversation.

29

USING BODY LANGUAGE

Level B1 – C1

Write these categories on the board:

- posture
- gestures
- physical distance
- facial expressions
- eye contact

Ask learners to give you definitions of these categories. They can give sentences such as *Posture is the position we hold our bodies in while standing or sitting.*

Brainstorm elements of body language with the class, such as movements with the hands, how people hold their heads while speaking or listening, smiles, frowns, etc. Ask learners what categories they think different types of body language falls into.

Put learners in groups to brainstorm the types of meanings that others get from these five elements of body language. For example, they can discuss what indicates different emotions such as interest, boredom, happiness, unhappiness, understanding, confusion, self-confidence, fear, etc.

Then ask the learners to create a short skit based on situations in the workplace. They act it out for the others, first using body language they feel is <u>inconsistent</u> with the text and then again with <u>consistent</u> body language. The others in the class then give feedback on how they experienced the skits.

Note: It is important to remind learners that we all have to be careful when analyzing body language. There may be another reason for the way someone is standing or sitting. For example, someone with their arms crossed may appear to be closed to an idea but in reality they may just be cold. Someone leaning too close might simply have difficulty hearing. This can also lead to a discussion of instances when body language was misinterpreted and how the learners dealt with it.

～

Real-world follow-up: Ask learners to notice body language in the workplace and to note down if they found it consistent with the verbal messages they heard or not. They can then talk about their observations in class.

30

CLARIFYING INFORMATION THROUGH QUESTIONS

Level B1+ – C2

We are often given information or instructions which are not clear but can be clarified by asking certain types of questions. These are several general categories of unclear communication.

Ask learners if they ever receive information which they are uncertain about. Then explain that it may simply be the way the information is put. Give them these categories and say that sentences falling into these categories often need further clarification. Read these out and ask learners to jot down notes about what they thing they might mean.

- Generalizations
- Vague statements
- Comparisons
- Judgments
- Unspecified nouns/pronouns
- Making assumptions

Before explaining these further, read out these sentences and ask learners to categorize them according to the categories you have given them. The answers follow in parenthesis.

1. *Europeans always use public transport.* (Generalizations)
2. *This is the best solution.* (Comparisons)
3. *I know you're not interested in this.* (Making assumptions)
4. *They are certainly right.* (Unspecified nouns/pronouns)
5. *Obviously, he knows what he's doing.* (Judgments)
6. *We have to improve communication.* (Vague statements)

When we hear statements like these, we often do not have enough information to react. Once we learn how to question them, however, we can receive more information.

Here are some sample questions for the examples above.

1. Generalizations: *Always? In every situation?*
2. Comparisons: *Best for whom? In what way is it the best solution?*
3. Making assumptions: *What specifically tells you I'm not interested? / How do you know that?*
4. Unspecified nouns: *Who is* they? */ Which people do you mean?*
5. Judgments: *What makes it obvious? Obvious to whom?*
6. Vague statements: *What exactly needs to be improved? What needs to be communicated, and to whom? How*

frequent should communication be, and how should it take place?

Ask the whole class to think of other sentences that fit the categories above and to come up with questions that help clarify the situation. Remind them that depending on the context, the follow-up questions may not be necessary, but when communication is not clear, these questions can save time and energy and lead the thinking process in new directions.

A word of warning: these types of questions can be overused and should only be used when the original sentence is truly unclear to the listener.

Reassure learners that it's often all right to begin their own speech or writing with a generalization or a vague statement, as long as they follow it up with specifics. Remind them to anticipate the kinds of clarification questions listeners or readers might ask and to address them.

∾

Real-world follow-up: Ask learner to notice comments like these in the workplace and to report back if an appropriate question helped to clarify the situation.

31

WORKING IN TEAMS

Level B1+ – C1

Ask learners if they can give some tips for working in teams. Collect as many as possible. Then explain that managing teamwork is a major part of working together, and often consists of turn-taking and active listening. Ask learners to think of phrases that they can use to indicate that they are finished speaking and that it's another person's turn; to check if someone was actively listening to the others; to indicate that they themselves understood what another person said. Write these on the board.

Some examples might be:

- *So,* (name), *what do you think?* (Active listening)
- *That's my opinion. Does anyone want to add something to this?* (Turn-taking)
- *I think we should ... Do you agree, or do you have another idea?* (Active listening and turn-taking)

- *My idea is to … Does anyone have anything to add?*
  (Active listening and turn-taking)

Put learners in small groups and ask them to choose a topic, or assign one to the group that they can all discuss. These can be general topics such as working overtime, parental leave, yearly raises, etc.

Tell them their job is to come up with a suggestion to present to the managing board, and they have 5 minutes to discuss what they would like to do. Ask one person to be an observer, and after 5 minutes ask the observers in the groups if everyone got the same amount of time to speak.

Then appoint a different person to be a 'turn-taking' monitor and arrange a non-verbal signal for this person to give the group if it is time for a different person to speak.

Have them continue with the conversation for another 5 minutes, with the monitor signaling if any members are dominating the discussion.

When they finish, ask how it went the second time and if there was any language they particularly noticed or felt they needed in order to guarantee that turn-taking took place.

As a final exercise, ask members of the group to repeat suggestions or ideas that others had and clarify with the group if all the topics were remembered and mentioned, to see how well team members used active listening techniques.

∾

Real-world follow-up: Make notes at work of situations in which people actively listened to others and when real turn-taking took place. Report back to the class about it.

32

THE DISNEY STRATEGY FOR CREATIVE SOLUTIONS

B2 – C2

Ask learners what they know about Walt Disney. Explain to them that the NLP (Neuro-Linguistic Programming) expert Robert Dilts, analyzed what helped Disney to be creative and divided the process into three areas:

- **Dreamer** (All dreams are valid; there are no restrictions; money or time or resources don't play a role.)
- **Realist** (Dreams cannot become reality unless they are practical; questions about cost, time frame, and available resources have to be clarified.)
- **Critic** (Once the dreamer and the realist have worked through an idea, it needs to be looked at again from the point of view of what could go wrong. It is necessary to consider the worst-case scenario and have a plan to deal with it if it happens.)

Lead a discussion on what the learners think these three areas could involve. Help them with ideas about the phases in coming up with a creative idea (answers in parentheses above).

Put learners into groups of 4-6. Ask them to come up with an idea and go through all three phases together as a group. Ask them to first go through a "blue-sky" thinking phase where anything is possible, then come up with specifics for carrying this out, and finally look at the possibilities for problems or disaster. Then go back to the original idea and refine it. The groups can present their ideas after all three phases have been discussed and agreed upon. Encourage others to ask questions about the process and discuss how easy or difficult it was for groups to come to an agreement.

Ideas taken from Robert Dilts, *Walt Disney, the Dreamer, The Realist and the Critic* (1995). Dynamic Learning Publications, Ben Lomond, CA, USA.

~

Real-world follow-up: Ask learners if there is a creative process in their workplace and if they have noticed anyone taking on these particular roles.

33

CULTURAL AWARENESS

Level B1 – C2

Ask learners if they have people from different cultures working in their companies. Ask them if they notice any specific customs or traditions.

Explain that cultural beliefs cannot always be seen but that there are a number above the surface while the underlying beliefs and values may be hidden below the surface. Brainstorm things that are done differently in different parts of the world. Here are some suggestions:

- Food and dining habits
- Families
- Attitude towards work
- Attitude towards authority
- Holidays
- Clothing
- Greeting and saying good-bye to people
- Small talk

- Team work
- Level of formality
- Risk-taking

Lead a discussion on customs that people in the class have. Ask if they have noticed differences between people in the workplace or business partners in other countries.

Put learners in groups and ask them to discuss the impact culture could have in the business world. Do any of the points mentioned have an effect in the workplace, and if so, how? Could they imagine spending time working in another country? Why or why not?

Then ask them to put together a short manual for someone coming from abroad to use when joining their company along with tips for those in the company to consider when they have guests or partners from other cultures. After they have finished, ask each group to briefly present their ideas to the others and discuss.

~

Real-world follow-up: Ask learners to look for any situations in the workplace in which culture played a part. Ask them if people were surprised or upset by the situation, or if everyone was understanding and worked through it.

34

GIVING AND RECEIVING FEEDBACK

Level B1+ – C1

In the workplace, we often have to give and receive feedback. Having an idea of what to say can make this easier.

Hold a brainstorming session on what makes feedback helpful and effective as well as what makes it ineffective and even harmful. Write some of the ideas on the board.

Then read aloud this questionnaire about a time they received feedback. Ask learners to make notes while listening.

1. Did you get useful information to help you work more successfully or efficiently in the future?
2. Have you received feedback that criticized your work, as well as feedback that praised it?
3. Did you feel that the person who gave you feedback had your wellbeing in mind?

4. Was the feedback specific? Did it focus on a particular situation or event?
5. Was the feedback given immediately following the event?
6. Were you asked to confirm that you understood what was said?
7. Was the feedback about the work you produced or about you as a person?

Now read these questions about learners' feelings while receiving feedback.

1. Did you try to stay calm and listen?
2. Did you accept the feedback as information?
3. Did you ask for more specifics?
4. Did you express your understanding of the feedback?

Lead a general, whole-class discussion on these aspects of receiving feedback. Ask them as well to talk about times when they felt feedback was not helpful and why; and times they learned from feedback and how they used the information they were given.

Next, go back to the first set of questions and ask learners to reformulate them so that they are about giving feedback to others (e.g., *Do you give others useful information to help them work more successfully or efficiently in the future?* or *How do you give information so that the other person can work more successfully or efficiently in the future?*). Have learners discuss in small groups these aspects of giving feedback. Ask them to reflect on what they said about receiving feedback; based on that, would they change anything in the way they give feedback, and if so, what?

The following link gives additional advice for using feedback.

https://baird-group.com/10-tips-for-giving-and-receiving-feedback-effectively/

∼

Real-world follow-up: Ask learners to make notes on feedback they give or receive at work, as well as their own reactions or the reactions of others, to share in future classes.

PART 6

BUSINESS SKILLS

These are often the bread-and-butter of the workday, and although learners may be confident in these techniques in their first language, many feel they need practice to gain confidence in English.

Point out that not having English as a first language can also be used to an advantage and may help learners to feel more secure because they can make use of techniques such asking others to speak more slowly or repeat what they had said in different words. They can also paraphrase the content or words themselves to give themselves more time and ensure they are not misunderstood by others.

35

NEGOTIATING

Level B2 – C2

Ask learners to name the situations in which they need to negotiate. Explain that there are certain tactics which can help them in these situations.

Brainstorm ideas for: (suggested answers are in parentheses)

- Asking for more time (*I see what you are saying, but we would need time to consider the possibilities / Could we arrange another meeting to discuss this more thoroughly?*)
- Making suggestions (*What do you think about this idea? / I would like to suggest that we ...*)
- Expressing one's needs (*I feel that we need to ... / We think it is vital to ...*)
- Expressing another perspective (*Could we look at this from our point of view? / Let's consider this from another perspective.*)

- Making compromises (*If we do this ..., can you ... ? / We would be happy to ..., if you ...*)
- Paraphrasing (*If I can put this in other words ... / So I think the gist of what we are discussing is ...*)
- Summing up the main idea (*I believe this is what we are now saying. / If I understood everything correctly, it is ...*)

Once learners have a number of phrases they can use, put them together in groups of four. Tell each group to come up with an idea that they can negotiate (flexible hours, a four-day workweek, working from home, etc.) Two of the people agree to negotiate with each other and two are asked to be observers.

Set a time limit of about three minutes. Then stop the groups and ask the observers to take over the negotiation after choosing which role they want to play. The original negotiators now observe for about three more minutes.

Stop the groups and ask the observers to give feedback to the negotiators. If the negotiation was not finished, ask if they thought each of the negotiators would leave feeling they had achieved their goals. If yes, why; and if no, why not?

∾

Real-world follow-up: Ask learners to report on the types of negotiations that take place in the workplace and how they are carried out. Ask for details on the language used and how often both sides seem to be satisfied when the negotiations are over.

36

GIVING PRESENTATIONS

Level B1+ – C2

Presentations generally are divided into parts. Elicit from the class what they think these parts are. Then give them this framework and begin to fill it in with phrases they can use.

- Greetings and introduction (*Good morning, welcome to … / My name is … and I am glad to see to see you all here.*)
- Preview (*Today I am going to tell you about … / In this talk, you are going to find out about …*)
- Body of the presentation (*We are going to start with … / Now I would like to move on to … / Next we'll address … / After that, I'll explain …*)
- Review (*Finally, I'd like to sum up what I said about … / To conclude, …*)
- Closing (*Thank you for your attention. / Are there any questions?*)

Mention that presentations often use what is called "signposting language" to indicate where people are at a specific point in the presentation. Ask learners to say which of the phrases above serve that purpose and brainstorm a few more, such as *at this point / first of all / secondly / next / following this / in conclusion / turning over to my colleague …*)

Then discuss phrases they can use in the body of the presentation to mention general information, details, and reasons: such as *basically / generally / in general / specifically / … is due to … / as a result … / in order to …*)

Next, discuss phrases to use in the question and answer period in case it is not possible to give an answer on the spot: *That's an interesting question; I'll have to get back to you. / Could you meet me afterwards so we can discuss this in detail? / I want to make sure I understand the question—are you saying …?*)

Finally, brainstorm presentation topics with the class and come up with at least one topic for each group of four to five. Put learners in their groups and ask them to come up with phrases or words that could be used for their topic. Then ask the group to put together a presentation on their topic and choose either one person or several people to give the presentation to the class.

The task for the rest of the class is to

- point out what they thought went well
- comment on good use of structure
- comment on good use of signposting language
- comment on the positive handling of questions

Real-world follow-up: Ask learners to pay attention to presentations they see in their workplace and notice if they include a structure and signposting language. Then have them share their observations with the class. If you wait till several learners have something to share, they can compare/contrast the different presentations in groups, and notice if there are any presentation styles or language that seem to be unique to their company.

37

MEETINGS

Level B1+ – C2

Ask learners how often they take part in meetings and if any of them are in English. Explain that certain phrases are used for different functions during a meeting.

Call out these phases and ask learners to say what they think the function of the phase is and to write them down.

- *It really depends.* (Being non-committal)
- *I think that …* (Giving a suggestion)
- *All in favor? / All opposed?* (Voting)
- *What do you think about … ?* (Asking for opinions)
- *I would like to open this meeting …* (Starting a meeting)
- *Going back over the main points …* (Summarlzing)
- *Could you explain that again?* (Clarifying)
- *I'm not convinced …* (Disagreeing)
- *If you would allow me to continue …* (Preventing an interruption)
- *Thank you all.* (Ending the meeting)

- *Could I just say something here?* (Interrupting)
- *Let's start with ...* (Putting things in order)
- *Absolutely.* (Agreeing)

Ask learners if they know other phrases that would fit these categories and ask them to write them down. Then put them in groups of at least 6 people and assign topics such as:

- Daily working hours - fixed or not fixed
- Benefits and perks (extra benefits) - should everyone get them
- Pay raises – automatic or based on achievements
- Overtime policies – paid or unpaid

Ask groups to choose one topic. Randomly assign numbers to the members of the group for these roles:

1. Meeting chair (in favor of whatever is best for the company)
2. Scribe (takes the minutes*)
3. Opposes the basic idea
4. Is in favor of the basic idea
5. Is unsure and waiting to be convinced
6. Does not want to express his/her own opinion but tries to side with the chair

*Explain that the minutes are often based on the agenda if there is one. This provides a clear structure for the minute-taker. In meetings which have looser agendas, the minutes-taker might ask specifically which parts should be included, or the chair might direct the minutes-taker during the meeting.

When the groups have finished, ask the scribes to share the minutes with the group and discuss if what the scribe wrote down is accurate. Discuss if the members felt the meeting was productive and why or why not. Ask if everyone got to take part or if anyone dominated the meeting.

~

Real-world follow-up: Ask learners to report back on meetings they attended recently.

38

STYLES OF WORKING

Level B1+ – C2

Styles of working play a role in how we react to situations at work and can lead to different approaches to tasks or conflicts if others don't understand why we react as we do. Work styles often are the reason behind our behavior or the language we choose to express ourselves. It is important to remember that these different approaches are not right or wrong, they are just explanations for why people react as they do.

Styles of working are often set up as opposites, and some people may always react in a certain way while others may move from one to the other. Here is a common list:

- Proactive – Reactive
- Internally oriented – Externally oriented
- Task-oriented – Relationship-oriented
- Options – Rules
- Big picture – Details

- Same – Different

Read out these short descriptions and ask learners to categorize the behavior. The answers are in parentheses.

- This person always knows when he or she is right and doesn't rely on the opinions of others. (Internally oriented)
- This person likes to get to know the members of a team before starting to work. (Relationship-oriented)
- This person asks for an overview of a project before wanting to know about the steps. (Big picture)
- This person looks for what is different in information or a task from previous information or tasks. (Different)
- This person waits until others have made suggestions before giving their opinion. (Reactive)
- This person likes many possibilities when approaching a new task. (Options)

Now ask learners to come up with similar descriptions to describe the other terms. Suggested answers are below.

- This person is the first to come up with ideas or proposals. (Proactive)
- This person often needs support from others when doing their job. (Externally oriented)
- This person gets to work on a task without taking time to get to know the others on the team. (Task-oriented)

- This person likes to have procedures to follow. (Rules)
- This person likes to know exactly what they have to do without having to consider the complete picture. (Details)
- This person looks for similarities to work they are familiar with when they are given new tasks to complete. (Same)

Put learners in small groups to discuss these characteristics and decide where they fit in. Have them talk about how this affects the workplace and if they have colleagues who work differently than they do. They should then discuss whether knowing this information gives them any insight into their colleagues' behavior and how this might affect their work in the future or help them be more tolerant of the way other people do things.

Next, try a role play. Put learners in groups of four: two actors and two observers. Each group chooses a typical workplace situation (e.g., handing in a report, running a meeting, discussing a deadline, etc.). The two actors also choose a work style, and then each assumes a different aspect of that style (e.g., one is relationship-oriented and the other is task-oriented). Let groups act this out for 3 – 4 minutes, then stop them and ask the observers for feedback. They then change places, choose another situation and working style, and do the role play again.

~

Real-world follow-up: Ask learners to look for specific examples in the workplace of conflicting working styles and report back on their observations in class.

39

EMOTIONAL INTELLIGENCE

Level B2 – C2

Emotional intelligence was an area that psychologists began discussing in the 1990s. Then in 1995 Daniel Goleman wrote a book on the subject that helped to make the concept more widely known. Soon business people realized that emotional intelligence also needed to be cultivated in the workplace.

"Emotional intelligence" has been defined as the ability to understand and control your own emotions as well as to understand the emotions of others; and has been recognized as being vital for teamwork or leadership positions. Having a high "EQ," or emotional intelligence quotient, helps business people give better feedback and receive it more easily, deal with challenging situations, work cooperatively in a team, and deal with stress and change in the workplace.

Give learners some of the background information above and explain that the factors of EQ are usually defined as below. Read them out and ask learners to write them down. Then ask them to come up with definitions of these factors. Suggestions are in parentheses.

- Self-control (Controlling your own reactions to situations and your emotions)
- Self-motivation (Being motivated to complete tasks without needing to receive praise from others)
- Empathy (Understanding how other people feel and being able to put yourself in their shoes)
- Social skills (Being able to talk easily to others, work with them cooperatively, establish rapport, and use appropriate non-verbal communication)

Ask the whole class to think about the four factors and give examples of these in the workplace. Discuss the situations in which they occurred and ask if those involved got the outcomes they had hoped for. Then lead a discussion on situations in which emotional intelligence was lacking and what outcomes came from those. Finish the discussion with suggestions for language that could be used in connection with the four factors.

Examples:

- Self-control: I'm not happy with the result, but there's no point in getting angry about it.
- Self-motivation: It's important to me to do a good job on this report, so I'm taking my time with it.

- Empathy: I understand how you feel. This must have been a difficult situation for you.
- Social skills: How is everything going? Are you settling in well in your new position?

~

Real-world follow-up: Ask learners to observe situations in the workplace in which EQ helped to solve a problem or where a lack of EQ made it worse.

40

SETTING ACHIEVABLE GOALS

Level B1+ – C2

Lead a whole class discussion on the importance of setting realistic goals. Ask learners if they have done this, and elicit tips from those who have been successful.

Present these steps in setting achievable goals and ask learners to comment on them. (If your learners need it, some further information in parentheses is provided after each statement.)

1. Start with a positive statement of what you would like to achieve. (It is easier to make a vision of something positive than something negative as the negative one only expresses what one doesn't want and not what they do. In addition, negative ideas may open the door to many alternatives but there is no guarantee that they are really what the person wants to achieve.)

2. Ask yourself if it is within your control. (Is this something that you alone have the power to achieve or do others have a great deal of influence on the feasibility of this goal?)
3. What evidence will you have that you have achieved it? (What will you see, hear, feel, etc. that tells you that you have reached your goal?)
4. Where and when do you want to achieve this goal? (Is there is specific time when or a specific place where you would like to achieve this? Also think about where you might not want to achieve it. (Sometimes work goals should stay at work and not be implemented in one's personal life, for example.)
5. How does this goal affect others? (Are there people in your life who will be affected – either negatively or positively – if you achieve your goal?)
6. Does the goal align with your values and beliefs? (Is this goal something that fits to who you are, to what you believe in and to what you find important?
7. When will you take the first step? (When exactly will you begin?)

Put learners in groups and ask one to name a work goal they would like to achieve. Tell the others to take the person through these steps. Remind them that sometimes an answer to a question may mean going back and revising the original goal. Give them 15 – 20 minutes to work on the exercise, then debrief and ask for feedback.

~

Real-world follow-up: Ask learners to think about goals they have had or others have had at work and if they have been reached or not. Ask them if any of these questions could have helped along the way.

41

GROWTH MINDSETS

Level B2 – C2

Ask learners these questions and give them time to respond.

1. Do you think we are born with a certain intelligence that cannot be changed?
2. Does learning new things have an effect on our intelligence?
3. Do you believe that people can change the type of person they are?
4. Do you enjoy a challenge, or do you usually avoid challenging situations?
5. Does fear of failure ever hold you back from trying new things?
6. Do you feel that you can make choices about things you want to do?
7. Do you often stretch out of your comfort zone?

Ask learners to make two columns on a piece of paper. One is labeled "Fixed mindset" (feeling that change is very difficult) and the other "Growth mindset" (feeling that change and growth are always possible). Ask them to work with a partner and jot down ideas about what they think belongs in each column. With the whole class, go over what they have written down. Here are some examples:

Fixed mindset (first column)

- Our intelligence is fixed, and we can't change it.
- Learning new things has no effect on our basic intelligence or abilities.
- We are a certain type of person and can't easily change.
- Challenges are too hard.
- If I am going to fail, there is no point in trying.
- I really don't have a choice in what I want to do or achieve.
- I prefer my comfort zone.

Growth mindset (second column)

- Our intelligence can change throughout our lives.
- Learning new things has an effect on our brains.
- We can change the type of person we usually are.
- I like challenges even if they are frightening.
- I might fail, but if I don't try, I will never know.
- I am responsible for my own choices.
- I often leave my comfort zone.

Next, lead a whole class discussion on fixed mindsets and growth mindsets and the effect these have in the workplace. Ask learners to give examples of situations where they felt they experienced the fixed mindset or the growth mindset, and the consequences of each.

Then lead the discussion to future events, and ask if anyone has ideas they want to try out or goals they would like to achieve using ideas from a growth mindset. Lead a discussion on specific steps they might take or ideas they have to incorporate growth into their future goals.

Ideas are from *Mindset*, Dr. Carol S. Dweck, Random House, NY, 2006.

∾

Real-world follow-up: Ask learners to observe situations in the workplace and note one that demonstrated a fixed mindset and one that demonstrated a growth mindset and report on these in class.

PART 7

USING AUTHENTIC MATERIALS

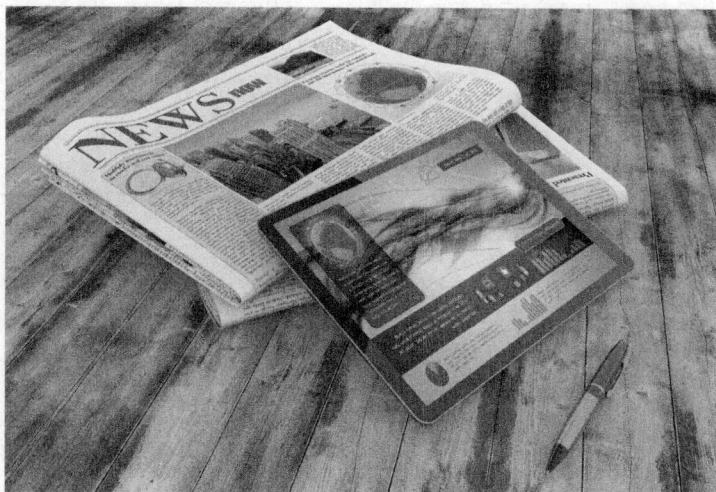

Learners often need to read websites, articles, company regulations, etc., and there are ways to make these tasks less daunting. This section will look at ideas and activities to use in class to help learners with the difficulties presented by authentic texts.

Since we are often expected to provide articles, here are some tips for finding materials. For example, look at the various business sections of online newspapers and magazines. Some of them are subscription only, but others are free to use or allow several articles a month to be downloaded. Several news sites (such as MSN, CBS, ABC, NBC, MSNBC, BBC) also have articles and videos on current events in the business world. Investopedia is an online business English dictionary that has longer texts as well. A good source of authentic videos are TEDTalks, which have a wide range of topics. Company websites also provide a wealth of vocabulary that learners may find very helpful.

42

PRE-TEACHING IMPORTANT VOCABULARY

Level B1+ – C2

Once you choose an article to use in class, go through it and pull out the vocabulary you feel your learners need to know in order to read it. There are several ways to pre-teach this vocabulary depending on how much time you have and how extensive the list is. Once the learners are familiar with the vocabulary, reading the text becomes much easier and satisfying for the learners.

Here are some teaching ideas for new vocabulary:

- Type out a list with the vocabulary on one side and on the other the translation into the mother tongue or a definition. The translations or definitions should be in a jumbled order. Ask learners to match the vocabulary words with their translations or explanations. Clarify any questions they have.
- Give learners a list of the vocabulary and go through the words to clarify meaning. Then put

learners in groups and ask them to write an article using the vocabulary you have given them. Have them read their articles aloud to the others.

- Write vocabulary words on cards with the explanations or translations on the back. Give one to each student. Have them mingle and ask their classmates if they know what the words mean; if not, the student with the translation or explanation gives them the answer. The leaners exchange cards and move on to other learners until everyone in the classroom has had each card.

- Put learners in groups and ask them to make gap texts or multiple choice texts for the others. Check their work and then have the groups exchange their texts with each other. The groups then get their original work back and correct it.

- Look for words that collocate with other words and have learners brainstorm as many as possible to build up a wider range of vocabulary. Point out that some words, e.g. *market* (*market research / target market*) can be the first or the second word in the collocation. Encourage them to build their vocabulary with collocations of words that come in articles they read.

- Advanced groups can also look for synonyms for some of the vocabulary used in the article and insert them instead. As synonyms sometimes have different connotations (negative or positive), this exercise can help learners understand why certain words are chosen for certain purposes.

Real-world follow-up Ask learners to find texts in English from their companies and look for new vocabulary words that they can explain to the others in the class.

43

UNDERSTANDING AUTHENTIC TEXTS

Level B1+ – C2

After working on the vocabulary, there are several activities that can be done with texts to aid comprehension.

Before reading:

- Before giving out the text, scramble the words in the title and ask learners to unscramble it. Then ask them to talk about what they think the text might be about.
- Create some questions on the topic of the text and ask learners their opinions. Get them to use some of the vocabulary in the discussion that was pre-taught.
- Give learners the gist of the text and ask them to write a list of words, phrases, or topics that they think will appear in the text. Have them check when they read the texts.

- Ask learners to write some questions they hope will be answered by the text.

During reading:

- Divide learners into groups and give each a part of the text. Then mix the groups, making sure that one person with each part of the text is in the new group and ask them to explain the part they read to the others.

After reading:

- Give learners multiple choice questions on the text and have them work in groups to answer them.
- Ask the learners to create gap texts or questions for each other based on the text. For more advanced groups, the gaps could be for synonyms for words that were in the text or questions that involve very careful reading.
- Create an exercise where learners mark sentences as true/false/not mentioned.
- Cut the text into bits. Leave several sentences together but make the last sentence incomplete. Hand out the pieces to the learners and ask the person who has the beginning piece read it aloud, come to the front of the room, and place it on a desk. Then the person who has the following piece does the same. Learners have to listen carefully to what is being read in order to know if their slip of paper is the logical continuation or not. Continue

until the entire text is complete. Remind the group that they are going to be asked questions after the text is put together so that those whose sentences came early on continue to listen. You can also give each learner two slips of paper (one from the first half of the text and one from the second) to guarantee listening for a longer period of time.

- Choose several words that could be added to the text—adjectives, adverbs, verbs, etc. Ask the learners to decide where in the text they should go.

- Set up a debate in which half the learners agree with the writer of the text and the other half disagree.

- Set up an interview in which a student interviews the writer of the text.

∿

Real-world follow-up: Ask learners to look for articles in their fields and compare what those say in relation to their own work situations or the companies they work for. Alternatively, if their companies produce any material in English, ask them to bring it to class and briefly talk about it.

44

USING COMPANY WEBSITES

Level B1+ – C2

Sometimes we have to help individual learners prepare for a business trip or a presentation to their own or another company.

One way to help them with this is to find the website of the company they work for as well as the website of the company they will be visiting. First determine which business area the learners need to discuss. Have a look at the website and try to find information relating to this. Print it out and bring it to the lesson. Go through this with the learners and work on phrases and individual vocabulary words that are new or difficult. Clarify any questions. You can also make use of the pre-reading activities mentioned in Tip #43 by making extra lists of vocabulary to pre-teach.

Run a simulation with learners by setting up the situation as it is expected to be. If you are teaching one-to-one, take part yourself as the business partner. If it is a class, assign roles, allowing the person who needs to prepare for the trip or the presentation to play themselves. Ask them to run the simulation without interrupting and take notes on what you think needs to be discussed afterwards.

When the simulation is over, give the learners notes. Tell them what went well, if there were any particulars you had trouble understanding, and clarify any miscommunication or vocabulary issues. Ask how they felt during the simulation and what they feel they still need to do in order to be prepared. If necessary, let them work on the vocabulary/presentation/communicative ideas at home and do a simulation again when you meet next.

$\sim$

Real-world follow-up: Ask learners how it went once they have had their meeting or presentation. Ask if there was anything else that would have helped them to prepare in case they need to do this again.

PART 8

GAMES AND ACTIVITIES

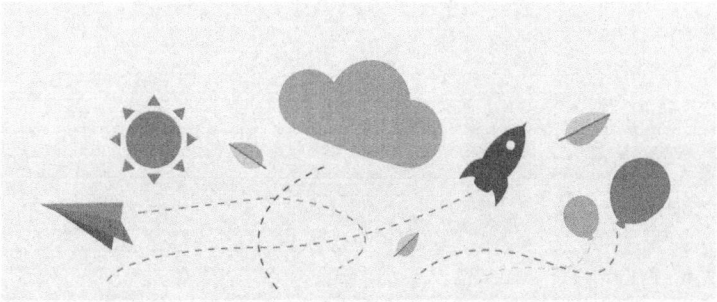

Business people often spend long days at the office working on their computers, attending meetings, listening to presentations, taking part in phone calls and teleconferences, and so on. When they come to English class, they are usually grateful for activities that are engaging, are different from their daily routine, allow them to use their creativity, and make language learning fun.

These activities can be used in a variety of settings and levels and deal with different vocabulary or aspects of work life. A number of them can be either prepared in advance or are completely learner-generated. In addition, they can be adapted to different groups and used as warm-up exercises, a break in the middle of a class or as a review.

45

ODD ONE OUT

Level B1 – C2

Most teachers are familiar with "odd one out" exercises, in which learners receive groups of words and have to choose the word they think does not belong. However, this can also be done by giving learners a group of words that are all more or less related to each other, and the learners have to explain why one word is slightly different from the others. The idea behind this is to choose words for the group that could all be the one that doesn't belong.

These can be created to practice specific vocabulary or done as a general activity for a group working in different fields. Although you may have specific ideas about what makes something different from the other items or terms, learners often come up with their own ideas, which encourages creativity and critical thinking and can enrich the conversation and help build confidence.

Some examples of these word groups and the reasoning behind the odd one out are:

1. Logistics / Dispatch / Distribution / Purchasing

All four words refer to the movement of goods or parts, but each word could be the odd one out.

- *Logistics* because it is carried out in the company and involves moving parts from one place to another.
- *Dispatch* because it involves packing products or parts and sending them to another branch or company.
- *Distribution* because it is a general term to describe sending goods or parts to those who need them.
- *Purchasing* because it involves receiving goods or parts rather than sending them.

2. Stapler / Glue / Paper clip / Hole punch

All four are office supplies, but each could be the odd one out.

- *Stapler* because something has to be added to it for it to work.
- *Glue* because each application of it can only happen one time.
- *Paper clip* because its shape can be changed.
- *Hole punch* because it is used to alter a piece of paper so that it can be put into a file folder.

An alternative idea is to put learners in groups and give them at least ten sets of words. Then ask them to write sentences describing the words but in a different order than the list of words. They can use phrasing such as "This word is different because ... " They then give their sentences to another group, who have to determine which sets of words the sentences describe.

The basic idea for this activity comes from *Games for Vocabulary Practice*, Felicity O'Dell and Katie Head, CUP, 2003.

∼

Real-world follow-up: Ask learners to think of four words dealing with their jobs that are related but that are also somewhere different from each other and bring them to class to discuss with the others.

46

GUESS MY WORD

Level B1 – C2

This activity works well to review vocabulary and to encourage learners to choose the vocabulary they want to practice.

Put learners in pairs of A and B. Ask each to write ten words they have learned on a piece of paper and number them one to ten. (Quickly check the lists to make sure each person has chosen ten different words.)

Tell learners that B is going to try to guess the ten words by asking questions. Give the groups a signal when five minutes are up. Then learners change places and A tries to guess the words B has chosen. The questions can be about the words (*Is this a noun?*), definitions (*Is this a small communication device used in and out of the office?*) or asking for specific responses (*When you meet someone for the first time, what do you say?*). One point is awarded for each word or phrase guessed.

When both people have finished, the words that were not guessed are revealed and the points are added up.

This activity can be helpful before an exam or simply to review vocabulary that was covered in class.

～

Real-world follow-up: Learners can create their own cards using words that are common in their workplaces and let their partner guess them.

47

TABOO GUESSING GAME

Level B1+ – C2

Create a set of cards with vocabulary you would like to review. Add four to six "taboo" words that learners are not allowed to use while describing the word.

Example of a card with taboo words / phrases:

---

word to guess: **desk**

taboo words: *office furniture, large, wooden, drawers*

Put learners in teams and give each team a set of cards. Members of each team take turns explaining the words—but not using any of the taboo words—to each other within a time frame of 60-90 seconds.

One person takes a card and tries to describe the word to their own team so they can guess it. The opposing team also needs to see the card so they can object if a "taboo" word is used. If the person describing uses a taboo word, the group has to stop and cannot continue guessing. If the describer's team guesses a word, they get a point. If they don't manage to do this in the time allotted, they can be told the word but get no point.

Then the second team has their turn to describe the words (without using the taboo words) so their teammates can guess. The winning group is the one with the most points.

An alternative is to have the teams make these cards for the other teams. You can give them each several words you feel need to be practiced, and they work together to add the taboo words. When each team has finished their cards, they exchange them with the other group, who has to explain them to their team members following the same rules as above.

~

Real-world follow-up: Learners can bring terms from the workplace to class and work with their teammates to create the cards for another group. You just need to make sure that the teams do not have any of the same words.

48

SHOUT IT OUT

Level A2 – C2

This idea is based on a popular game (Outburst) but has been adapted to the BE classroom.

Before class, decide on general topics that have been covered in past lessons, such as jobs in a particular sector, office supplies or furniture, departments in a company, adjectives to describe products, marketing or finance terms, or even topics such as what people like or dislike about their jobs.

Choose ten to twelve topics so that you have five or six each for two separate groups. Write the headings out and give them to the groups who work together to find five words that fit under the headings. For example, under the heading *office furniture* they could write *desk, filing cabinet, chair, table,* and *cupboard,* and under *departments* they could write *Marketing, HR, Production, Dispatch,* and *Customer Service.*

Put the class into two groups, A and B, and tell them they have to guess the words the other groups chose in one minute. The first group (A) reads just the heading out and group B shouts out words. If Group B gets a word on Group A's list, Group A checks it off. Use a timer and stop the guessing when time is up. Then ask Group B to read out the words on their lists that were missed. Group B gets one point for each word they guessed, and Group A gets two points for each word that wasn't guessed. Then Group B reads out a heading and Group A tries to guess the words. Continue until all the headings have been read and the words guessed. Add up the points.

Although learners only guess words, this activity expands their vocabulary in certain areas. As the teacher, you can choose the headings to practice that you know will be useful for your learners.

~

Real-world follow-up: Ask learners to think about words on a particular topic they need at work. They can jot them down and bring them to class and let the others guess what they are.

49

CREATE A COMPANY

Level B2 – C2

This game is a good way to start off a business English course as it involves talking about companies, what they do, and their structures.

Tell the class that half the class is going to make up a company and decide what it produces or provides as well as where it is located, how large it is, etc.

Divide the class in half and go out of the room with half of the class (Group A). Once the door is closed, tell Group A that they are *not* actually going to come up with an idea for a company but instead have to choose a "code" that determines how they answer the questions. For example, they may decide on the order of replies such as "Yes, no, no," or answer questions from people wearing glasses with "Yes" and the others with "No." The only time they can deviate is if they are asked a question that only makes sense with a negative or positive answer even if it breaks the code. An example would be if they answered a question such as *Are you a bank?* with *Yes*, and the next question is *Do you offer financial services?* According to a "Yes, no, no" code, the answer would have to be *No*; but that would make no sense, so the group is allowed to change it to *Yes*. Leave them to work out what their code will be. If the group is large, this group can be divided into two or three smaller groups so that each has a maximum of 4-5 people.

Then help Group B inside the room to come up with questions that can be answered with "Yes" and "No" responses. These can be simple ones like, "Are you located in the USA?" "Do you have more than 1000 employees?" etc. Help them come up with about ten questions. This group can be divided as well after the questions have been brainstormed.

The next step is to invite those outside back in the room and make groups of A's and B's. Tell those in Group B to start asking their questions, which Group A should answer following the code they decided on. Encourage Group B to take notes to help them guess. After a time, stop the groups and ask Group B what type of company they think Group A has formed. Then explain the "trick" and ask the students from A and B to now devise a company based on where the questions lead them.

These fictional companies can then be used to teach structure, jobs, department terminology, finance, marketing, etc., and can be used throughout the semester or the course.

Note: I learned the basics of this activity from Sheelagh Deller at a conference and added in the part about working on questions with Group B and continuing with the idea of a company throughout the course.

∽

Real-world follow-up: At the beginning of the course, learners could have others guess what type of company they work for using the same questions that they devised for the activity.

DRAW, ACT, EXPLAIN

Level A2 – C2

This activity is a children's game that works as an excellent review of vocabulary and phrases at the end of a course.

Look through the material you have taught and choose twenty or thirty terms you would like to review. Decide if the terms lend themselves to being drawn, acted out, or explained. Write the terms on individual cards or pieces of paper, and on the opposite side write "D" (for *draw*), "A" (for *act*), or "E" (for *explain*). Divide the cards in half making sure that each group has more or less the same number of drawing, acting and explaining terms.

In class, divide the class into two groups, A and B, and give each a pack of cards. Group A starts by one person taking a card and, after showing the other group the term, drawing or acting or explaining the word to his or her team members, who try to guess it within 1 minute. If the group doesn't guess it, the person with the card tells them what the word was. Then Group B does the same, and the game continues until all the words have been guessed. Each group gets points for the words guessed.

～

Real-world follow-up: Learners can create their own set of cards with vocabulary from the workplace and play the game with others in class, who have to guess them.

51. BONUS ACTIVITY
WORK-LIFE BALANCE

Level B1 – C1

Begin a discussion with learners about their understanding of the term "Work-life balance." Ask these questions and let them discuss them in groups:

- How do you define work-life balance?
- Why is it considered important?
- What steps can you take to achieve it?

After learners have discussed their ideas, lead a general class discussion on tips people have for staying focused at work but leaving work behind when the day is done. Ask people what they do to make the transition between the workday and their private lives, as well as how they keep work and their private lives separate. Write up some of the tips on the board.

Ask learners to make a list of priorities and rank them. Have them count them up and give feedback on whether the majority of their priorities deal with work or with their private lives.

Then move on to a discussion about what learners feel they need to cope—can they exercise, eat healthy food, get enough sleep, spend enough time relaxing, take short breaks during the work day, etc.?

End the activity by asking learners to think about again about their list of priorities and to take the time to consider possible changes.

∼

Real-world follow-up: Ask learners to keep a diary for a week or two, noting how much time they spend at work or thinking about work and how much time they spend doing free-time activities, and mark these activities as stressful or relaxing. These can then be discussed in class.

RESOURCES AND ACKNOWLEDGEMENTS

Charvet, Shelle Rose. *Words that Change Minds* (2019). Kendall / Hunt, Dubuque, USA.

Dweck, Carol S. *Mindset* (2017). Random House, New York, USA.

Goleman, Daniel. *Emotional Intelligence: Why It Can Matter More Than IQ* (2020). Random House, New York, USA.

Laborde, Genie Z. *Influencing with Integrity* (2012). Syntony, Mountain View, USA.

McCarthy, Michael; McCarten, Jeanne; Clark, David; Clark, Rachel. *Grammar for Business* (2010). Cambridge University Press, Cambridge, UK.

O'Connor, Joseph and Seymour, John. *Introducing Neuro-Linguistic Programming* (2011). Mandela, London, UK.

Rosenberg, Marjorie. *Communicative Business English Activities* (2018). Express Publishing, Newbury, UK.

Printed in Dunstable, United Kingdom